Union Public Library
1980 Morris Avenue
Union, N.J. 07083

P9-DBT-130

Looking Closely
along the Shore

FRANK SERAFINI

Union Public Library
1980 Morris Avenue
Union, N.J. 07083

Kids Can Press

Look very closely.

What do you see?

A flower?
A fossil?
What could it be?

It's a Common Sand Dollar.

This coinlike disc isn't actually a dollar. It is the skeleton of an animal called the common sand dollar.

When alive, sand dollars are covered with tiny hairs. Holes are arranged like flower petals on top of each sand dollar. The sand dollar pushes seawater in and out of these holes to move itself along the ocean bottom.

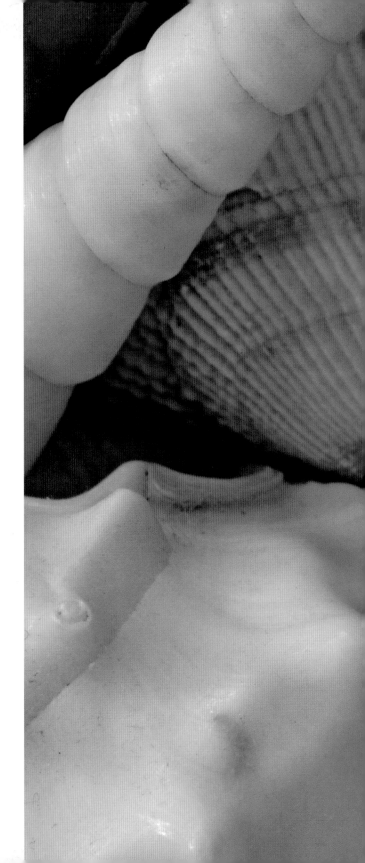

Look very closely.

What do you see?

Bird beaks?
Sunflower seeds?
What could it be?

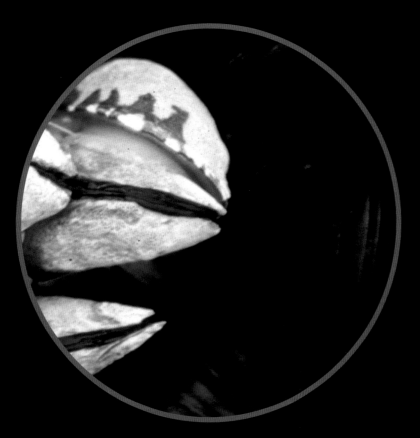

It's a Gooseneck Barnacle.

Barnacles cling to hard surfaces in the ocean, such as rocks, driftwood and sometimes the bottoms of boats. They live in groups where the waves crash along the shore.

Gooseneck barnacles keep their shells closed unless they are eating. When the tide comes in, the barnacles use their featherlike legs to sweep food into their stomachs. When the tide goes out, gooseneck barnacles tightly seal their shells to stay wet.

Look very closely.

What do you see?

Fish scales?
Sea snakes?
What could it be?

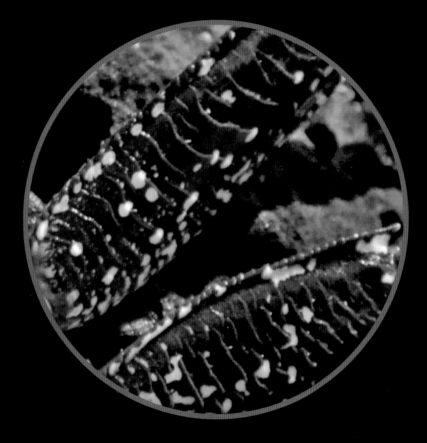

It's a Lined Shore Crab.

A shore crab has two claws, eight legs and a skeleton on the outside of its body. This hard shell is like a suit of armor. It protects the crab's soft body from seagulls and other predators.

The lined shore crab dances sideways along the shore. It squeezes into the cracks of rocks when it gets scared. Spots and lines on its back help the lined shore crab blend into the rocks to avoid being seen — and eaten!

Look very  closely.

What do you see?

Stars in the sky?
A handful of beads?
What could it be?

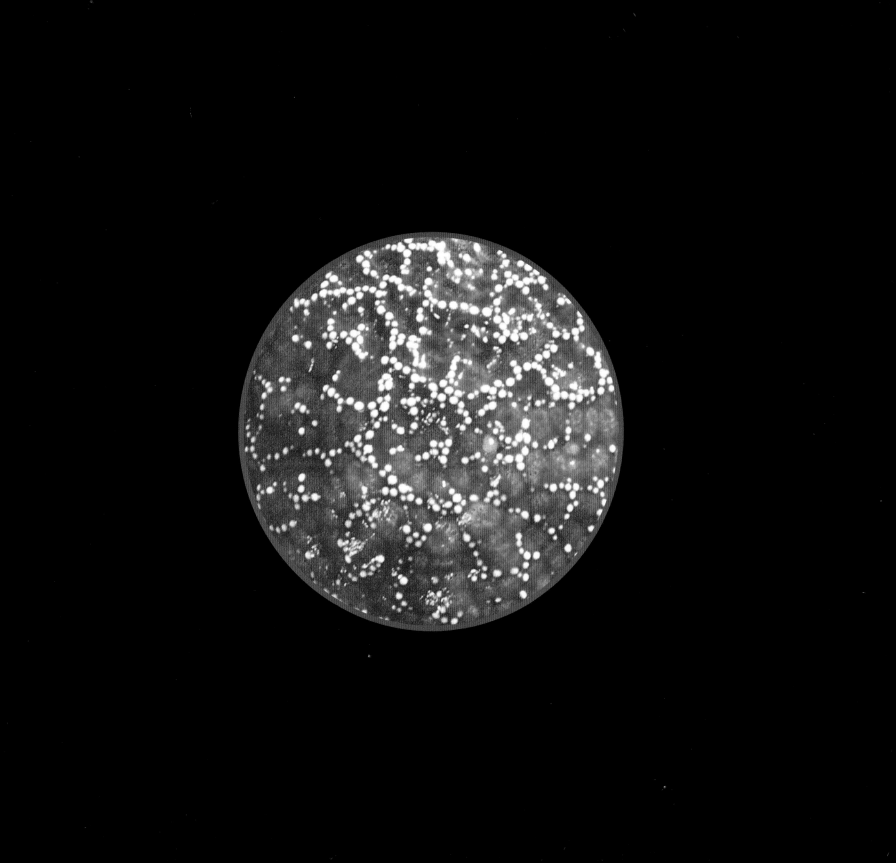

It's an Ochre Sea Star.

Over 2000 kinds of sea stars live in the world's oceans. Some people call them starfish, but they are not fish at all. Sea stars belong to the same family as sea urchins. Both animals have tough, spiny skin.

Some of the white points on the ochre sea star are pinchers. The sea star uses them to protect itself and keep plants and animals off its body.

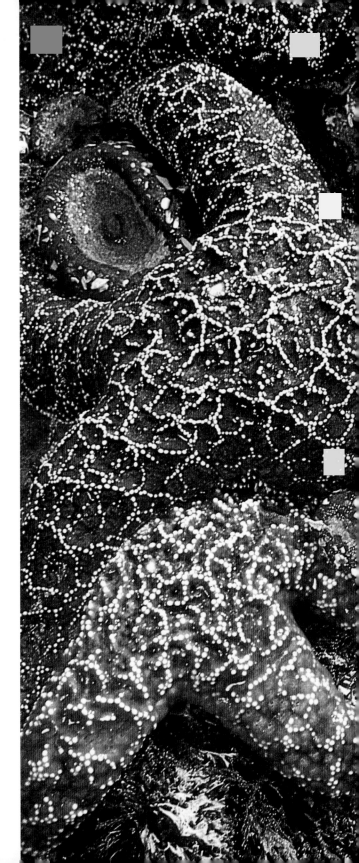

Look very closely.

What do you see?

Blades of grass?
Mermaid hair?
What could it be?

It's a Coconut Palm Tree.

Palm trees grow in warm or tropical places. They hang over the beach and sway in the ocean breeze. There are many kinds of palm trees. One you might know is the coconut palm tree.

Coconut palm trees have the biggest leaves of any plant in the world. The leaves sprout like giant fans from the treetop. Coconut palm trees also grow the world's biggest seeds. You have probably eaten them — they are called coconuts.

Look very closely.

What do you see?

Moon rocks?
A whale's mouth?
What could it be?

It's a Blue Mussel.

Mussels live in groups for protection. They have a tangle of threads called a beard that anchors them to rocks below the shoreline.

Like clams, mussels have two shells joined by a hinge. Blue mussel shells can be blue, black or purple with circle patterns on the outside. On the inside, they are white and smooth as a pearl.

Look very closely.

What do you see?

Whipped cream?
A shark tooth?
What could it be?

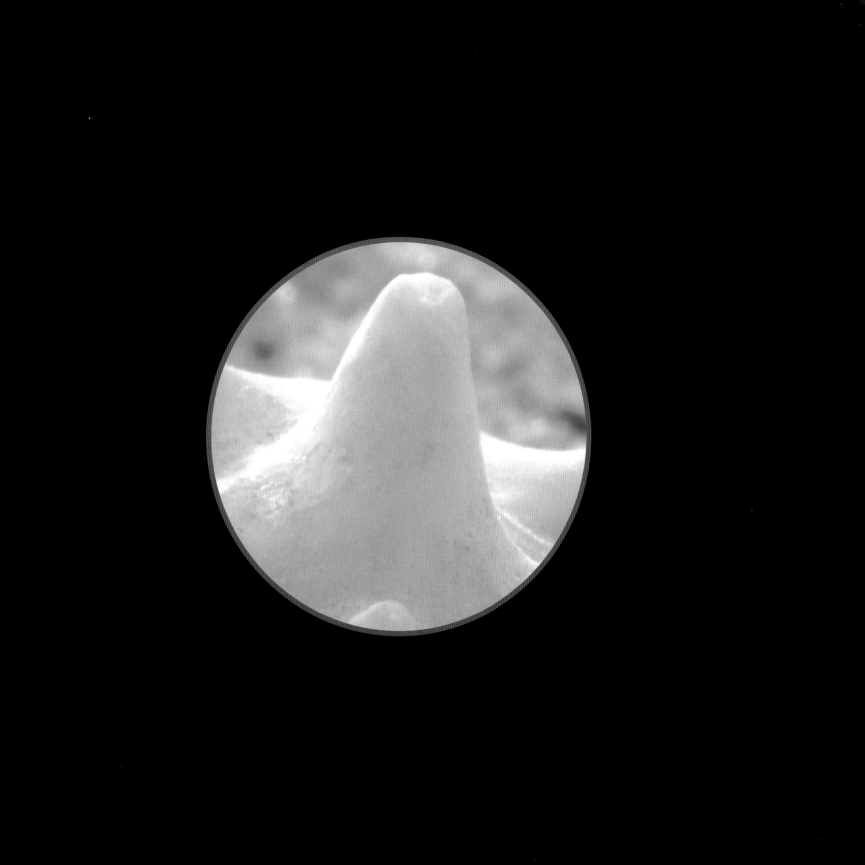

It's a Queen Conch Shell.

Queen conch shells are some of the biggest of all seashells. They are made by an animal called the queen conch (say it "konk"). Queen conchs live in warm, shallow seas. They travel very slowly and bury into the sand to hide.

The queen conch uses minerals from the ocean water to make its shell. At the top of its shell is a spiral shape, called a whorl. The whorl of a queen conch shell always spins to the right.

Look very closely.

What do you see?

Green eels?
Monster fingers?
What could it be?

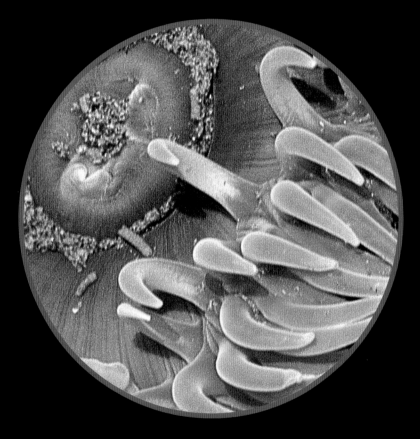

It's a Giant Green Sea Anemone.

Anemones are often called the "flowers of the sea." They are related to sea coral and jellyfish. But anemones are animals, not plants. They have a single foot that they use to attach themselves to ocean rocks.

The giant green sea anemone uses its tentacles to sting small fish and pull them into its mouth. When the tide goes out, the anemone tucks in its tentacles so they won't dry up.

Look very closely.

What do you see?

A marble?
A planet?
What could it be?

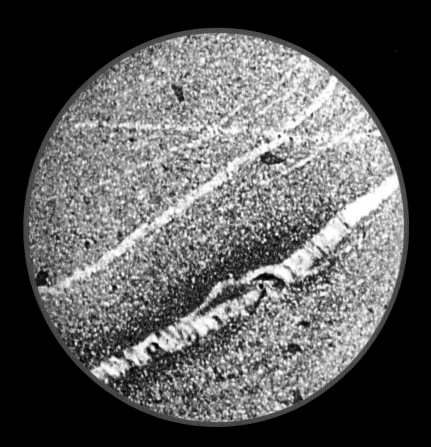

It's a Coastal Rock.

Some shorelines are covered with rocks instead of sand. Most coastal rocks were formed by sand, mud and broken seashells millions of years ago. If you look very closely, you can still see stripes of these minerals in the rocks.

Coastal rocks are worn smooth by crashing waves and drifting sand. It takes thousands of years to polish them this way.

To my nieces, Chandler and Morgan. May the pace of your lives always allow you to wander and wonder.

Photographer's Note

Photographers pay attention to things that most people overlook or take for granted. I can spend hours wandering along the shore, through the forest, across the desert or in my garden, looking for interesting things to photograph. My destination is not a place, but rather a new way of seeing.

It takes time to notice things. To be a photographer, you have to slow down and imagine in your "mind's eye" what the camera can capture. Ansel Adams said you could discover a whole life's worth of images in a six-square-foot patch of Earth. In order to do so, you have to look very closely.

By creating the images featured in this series of picture books, I hope to help people attend to nature, to things they might have normally passed by. I want people to pay attention to the world around them, to appreciate what nature has to offer, and to begin to protect the fragile environment in which we live.

Text and photographs © 2008 Frank Serafini

Pages 38–39: Taveuni, Fiji   Back cover: Malolo Lailai, Fiji

All rights reserved. No part of this publication may be reproduced, stored in a retrieval system or transmitted, in any form or by any means, without the prior written permission of Kids Can Press Ltd. or, in case of photocopying or other reprographic copying, a license from The Canadian Copyright Licensing Agency (Access Copyright). For an Access Copyright license, visit www.accesscopyright.ca or call toll free to 1-800-893-5777.

Kids Can Press acknowledges the financial support of the Government of Ontario, through the Ontario Media Development Corporation's Ontario Book Initiative.

Published in Canada by
Kids Can Press Ltd.
29 Birch Avenue
Toronto, ON M4V 1E2

Published in the U.S. by
Kids Can Press Ltd.
2250 Military Road
Tonawanda, NY 14150

www.kidscanpress.com

Edited by Karen Li
Designed by Julia Naimska
Printed and bound in China

This book is smyth sewn casebound.

CM 08 0 9 8 7 6 5 4 3 2 1

Library and Archives Canada Cataloguing in Publication

Serafini, Frank
Looking closely along the shore / Frank Serafini.

(Looking closely)
ISBN 978-1-55453-141-7

1. Seashore biology—Juvenile literature. I. Title.
II. Title: Along the shore. III. Series: Looking closely
(Toronto, Ont.)

QH95.7.S425 2008   j578.769'9   C2007-902574-9

Kids Can Press is a **corus** Entertainment company